THE WILD WORLD OF ANIMALS

KOALAS

MARY HOFF

CREATIVE EDUCATION

Special thanks to Dr. David Kay and Dr. John Rodger, University of Newcastle, New South Wales, Australia.

Published by Creative Education, 123 South Broad Street, Mankato, Minnesota 56001. Creative Education is an imprint of The Creative Company. Designed by Rita Marshall. Production design by The Design Lab. Photographs by Alamy (ACE STOCK LIMITED, David Wall), Corbis (Theo Allofs, Yann Arthus-Bertrand, Bettmann, Tom Brakefield, L. Clarke, DiMaggio/Kalish, Martin Harvey; Gallo Images, Chris Hellier, Eric and David Hosking, Hulton–Deutsch Collection, Simon Kwong/Reuters, Michael Maconachie; Papilio, Paul A. Souders, Gerry Whitmont/Australian Picture Library), Getty Images (Joseph J Scherschel), kevinschafer.com. Printed in the United States of America. Library of Congress Cataloging-in-Publication Data: Hoff, Mary King. Koalas / by Mary Hoff. p. cm. — (The wild world of animals). Includes bibliographical references and index. ISBN 1-58341-351-0. 1. Koala—Juvenile literature. I. Title. II. Wild world of animals (Creative Education). QL737.M384H64 2004. 599.2'5—dc22. 2004055264. First edition 9 8 7 6 5 4 3 2 1

It's a cool July evening in the mountains of New South Wales, Australia. High in the branches of a **eucalyptus** tree, a brownish gray animal is curled up, asleep. As the sun sets, her eyes open. She stretches and lifts her black nose to sniff the air. Behind her, a smaller nose sniffs, too. After a while, the mother koala begins nibbling the leaves around her. She moves from branch to branch with the baby riding on her back, sampling the **pungent** leaves. Half an hour later, their bellies are filled, and the two snuggle up for a nap.

Koalas look like cute teddy bears but aren't bears at all **5**

TREES, TOES, AND TEETH

Round-bodied and thick-coated, koalas are the furballs of Australian forests. They live in the eastern part of the continent. Some are found in the mountains, and others live on flat land. Other animals that live high in the trees with them include pythons, termites, jumping spiders, and birds known as kookaburras.

Koalas come in many sizes, with adults weighing from 11 to 31 pounds (5–14 kg). Males are bigger than females. Koalas that live in the south are bigger than those that live in the north.

Koalas are among the largest tree-dwelling mammals **7**

Koalas spend most of their time in eucalyptus trees. They eat almost nothing except eucalyptus leaves, bark, and fruit. A koala has many **adaptations** that help it live this unusual life.

A koala's coat helps it survive. In the cool south, the fur is thick and woolly. It keeps the koala warm and provides shelter from the rain. The color of a koala's fur

A koala's thick fur cushions it against tree bark

helps it hide from **predators**. Koalas in
the north are silver-gray with white on
their ears, arms, and chest. Those in the
south are darker—brownish gray with
white ears, arms, and chest.

Koalas eat only a few of the 600 types of eucalyptus **9**

Koalas' feet are perfect for climbing and clinging. Each front paw has two thumbs. The paws have rough bottoms and strong claws that help koalas grip tree branches. Koalas' toes leave fingerprints, just as human fingers do. Koalas' eyes are in front of their heads, rather than on the sides. This helps them judge how far away something is—a valuable skill when living far above the ground!

Koalas' strong arms and paws help them grasp branches **11**

Koalas have a good sense of smell. They use it to choose the best eucalyptus leaves to eat. A koala's sharp front teeth help it pull the leaves into its mouth. The back teeth grind the leaves. A space between the front and back teeth, called the "diastema," provides room for chewing. Koalas also have cheek pouches that allow them to have lots of food in their mouths at one time. Most animals have a hard time **digesting** eucalyptus leaves, but koalas don't have any trouble. They have special **bacteria** in their **intestines** that help them digest the leaves.

Their big noses help koalas find the tastiest leaves

If you spent your life roaming around in trees, how would you keep track of your babies? Koalas, like kangaroos and other marsupials, carry their young in a pouch on their belly. The pouch lets the mother koala use all four paws for climbing and still take her baby with her wherever she goes.

A mother koala's pouch opens toward her hind legs **15**

LIFE AS A KOALA

Eat and sleep, eat and sleep—that's the life

of a koala. Koalas eat 7 to 18 ounces (200–

500 g) of eucalyptus leaves every day. But

eucalyptus doesn't provide much energy.

Koalas get so little energy from the leaves

that they need to spend 18 to 20 hours each

day resting.

16   The fork of a tree is the perfect place for a nap

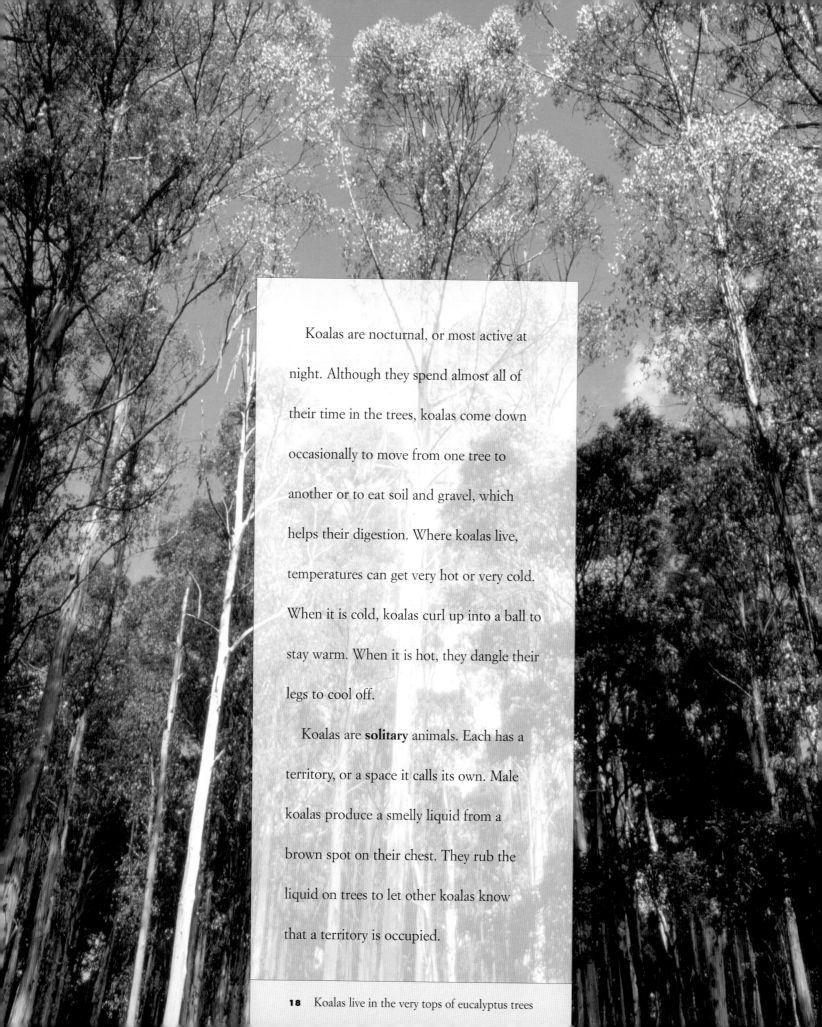

Koalas are nocturnal, or most active at night. Although they spend almost all of their time in the trees, koalas come down occasionally to move from one tree to another or to eat soil and gravel, which helps their digestion. Where koalas live, temperatures can get very hot or very cold. When it is cold, koalas curl up into a ball to stay warm. When it is hot, they dangle their legs to cool off.

Koalas are **solitary** animals. Each has a territory, or a space it calls its own. Male koalas produce a smelly liquid from a brown spot on their chest. They rub the liquid on trees to let other koalas know that a territory is occupied.

18   Koalas live in the very tops of eucalyptus trees

Koalas are born in spring and summer. A mother usually has one baby at a time. It is tiny—about as big as a jelly bean. The baby, called a "joey," crawls into its mother's pouch. The joey lives in the pouch, drinking milk and growing. When it is about six months old, the joey leaves the pouch. It clings to its mother's fur as she moves from branch to branch. Joeys stay with their mothers for about a year.

When the joey is ready for more than milk, its mother begins producing a soft food called "pap" from her **anus**. Pap contains helpful eucalyptus-digesting bacteria for the joey's intestines.

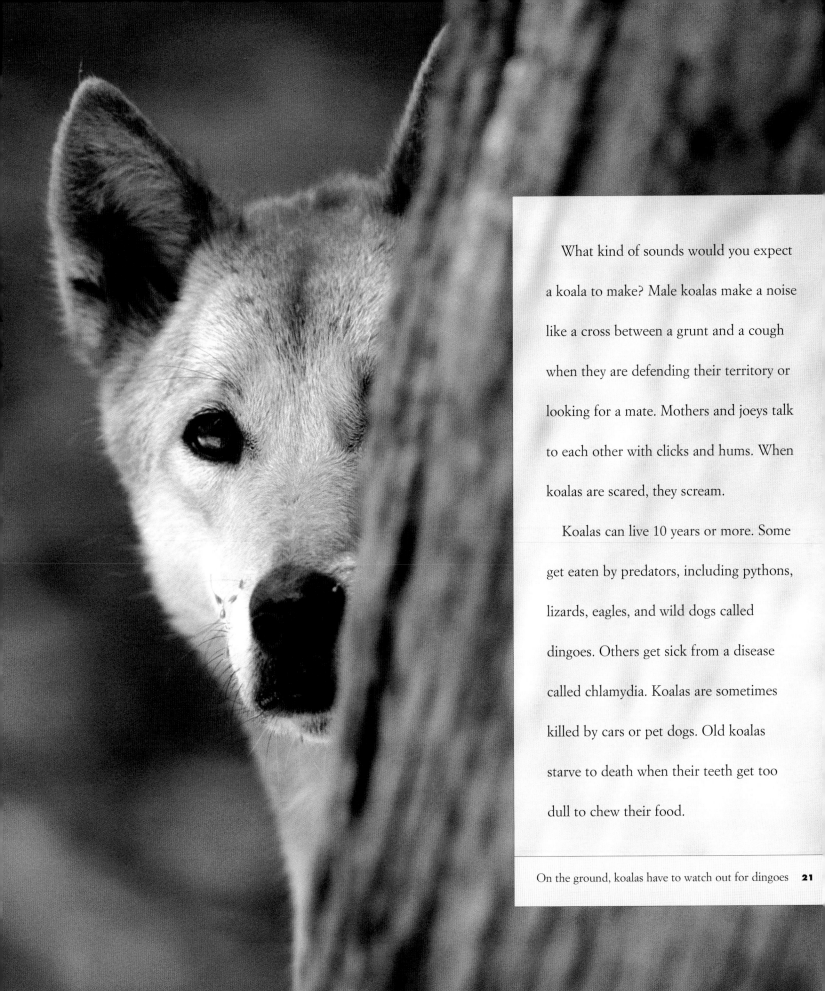

What kind of sounds would you expect a koala to make? Male koalas make a noise like a cross between a grunt and a cough when they are defending their territory or looking for a mate. Mothers and joeys talk to each other with clicks and hums. When koalas are scared, they scream.

Koalas can live 10 years or more. Some get eaten by predators, including pythons, lizards, eagles, and wild dogs called dingoes. Others get sick from a disease called chlamydia. Koalas are sometimes killed by cars or pet dogs. Old koalas starve to death when their teeth get too dull to chew their food.

On the ground, koalas have to watch out for dingoes

KOALAS AND PEOPLE

Humans and koalas have been part of each other's lives for thousands of years. Long before people from Europe began to settle in Australia in the late 1700s, koalas contributed to the survival of **Aborigines**, who captured the slow-moving animals for food.

Although Aborigines ate koalas, they also respected them and told stories about them. One legend explains why the koala has no tail. Another tells about an

22   Australian Aborigines shared the land with koalas

agreement Aborigines made with koalas in ancient times. In the story, people skinned koalas before they cooked them, which made the koalas so angry that they stole the people's water. Eventually, the thirsty people agreed to show respect for the koalas by not skinning them. In return, the koalas agreed not to take water away from the people anymore.

The Aboriginal word for koala means "no drink" **23**

After Europeans arrived in Australia, they destroyed eucalyptus forests to build homes and farms. Koalas had a harder time finding places to live. People also started hunting koalas for their **hides**. Millions of koala hides were sold in Europe and America to make clothing. By the early 1900s, koalas had disappeared from some parts of Australia.

24 Nearly 80 percent of eucalyptus forests have been destroyed

In the 1930s, koala hunting was made illegal. Instead of a source of hides, koalas became a symbol of Australia. Tourists looked for koalas when they visited Australia. Koala pictures were printed on stamps and coins. In 1971, the koala became the official animal symbol of the Australian state of Queensland.

Koalas are one of Australia's most popular animals **26**

Today, wildlife experts estimate that there are about 100,000 koalas living in the wild. Koalas are abundant in some parts of Australia. On one island there are so many koalas that people worry they will eat all the eucalyptus leaves and then starve. In other areas of Australia, there are no koalas at all.

Australia's forests once held millions of koalas   **29**

As Australians cut down more eucalyptus forests to build houses and roads, it will become even more difficult for koalas to find places to live. Fortunately, many people in Australia and around the world are trying to help koalas survive. They are working to set aside eucalyptus forests as parks and nature **reserves**. If people continue to care, these unusual little Australian animals will continue to thrive.

30   Koalas need eucalyptus trees to survive

GLOSSARY

Aborigines are dark-skinned, native people of Australia.

Adaptations are things about a plant or animal that help it survive where it lives.

The **anus** is the hole in an animal's body where its droppings come out.

Bacteria are single-celled living things that are all around us but are too small to see.

Digesting food is breaking it down so the body can use the energy it provides.

Eucalyptus is a strong-smelling evergreen tree that grows in Australia.

Hides are the skins of animals, often used to make clothing.

Intestines are the long, hollow tubes into which food goes after it leaves the stomach. They help digest the food.

Predators are animals that kill and eat other animals.

A **pungent** plant is one that has a strong odor or taste.

Reserves are areas of land set aside to provide a place for animals to live.

Solitary animals spend most of their time by themselves or with just their young.

BOOKS

Green, Carl R. *The Koala*. Berkeley Heights, N.J.: Enslow Publishers, 2003.

Lee, Sandra. *Koalas*. Chanhassen, Minn.: The Child's World, 1998.

Wexo, John Bonnett, Walter Stuart, and Karel Havlicek. *Koalas and Other Australian Animals*. Poway, Calif.: Zoobooks, 1997.

WEB SITES

Australia Down Under: Koalas http://www.saczoo.com/3_kids/1_australia/koalas.htm

Kids' Planet: Koala http://www.kidsplanet.org/factsheets/koala.html

National Geographic.com Kids http://www.nationalgeographic.com/kids/creature_feature/0008/koalas.html

INDEX